Bla
an
She's Leaving Home

Plays for Young People

Methuen Drama's Plays for Young People series
offers an excellent selection of single plays and anthologies
aimed at young people to perform. The series features
the highest-quality work by established playwrights,
which is age-appropriate and organised into age bands
to help teachers and youth theatre leaders select
the most suitable for their group.

Keith Saha

Black

and

She's Leaving Home

methuen | drama

LONDON • NEW YORK • OXFORD • NEW DELHI • SYDNEY

METHUEN DRAMA

Bloomsbury Publishing Plc
50 Bedford Square, London, WC1B 3DP, UK

BLOOMSBURY, METHUEN DRAMA and the Methuen Drama logo
are trademarks of Bloomsbury Publishing Plc

First published in Great Britain 2018

Series design: Louise Dugdale
Cover design: Olivia D'Cruz
Cover image © iStock/archideaphoto

A catalogue record for this book is available from the British Library

A catalog record for this book is available from the Library of Congress

ISBN: PB: 978-1-3500-8519-0
ePDF: 978-1-3500-8520-6
eBook: 978-1-3500-8521-3

Series:: Plays for Young People

Typeset by Country Setting, Kingsdown, Kent CT14 8ES
Printed and bound in Great Britain

To find out more about our authors and books visit
www.bloomsbury.com and sign up for our newsletters.

Black/She's Leaving Home

Keith Saha is Co-Artistic Director of 20 Stories High. He started out in the Everyman Youth Theatre in Liverpool before going on to be an actor, working for companies such as Cardboard Citizens, Contact, Graeae, Red Ladder and Birmingham Rep. He then became a composer and musical director for theatre before focusing on being a playwright and director. Since setting up 20 Stories High in 2006, he has been focusing on writing and developing a wide variety of plays using different forms including spoken word and verbatim theatre; and pioneering the form of hip-hop theatre with puppetry and mask. In 2010, he was awarded the Brian Way Award for the UK's Best New Play for Young People for his play *Ghost Boy*, a co-production with Contact and Birmingham Rep, which championed this form, and more recently his play *The Broke 'n' Beat Collective* won the Young Critics' Award at ASSITEJ: On the Edge Festival 2016. He is currently developing his writing for TV and film.

20 Stories High was founded in 2006, and has established itself as one of the leading young people's theatre companies in the UK. They collaborate with working class and culturally diverse young people, emerging and established artists to tell stories that are . . .

gritty, jumping, melodic, rebellious,
contemporary, mashed-up, authentic, original,
visual, challenging, lyrical, tender,
anarchic, diverse, surprising, booming,
political, funny, collaborative and heart-felt

They believe that . . .

everybody's got a story to tell . . . and their own way of telling it . . .

In 2016 *The Broke 'n' Beat Collective* (Keith Saha/Sue Buckmaster) won the ASSITEJ Festival of Theatre for young audiences Young Critics' Award, and 20 Stories High won the National Theatre's Jenny Harris Award for work with Young People. In 2013 *Whole* (Philip Osment) won the Writer's Guild of Great Britain Young People's Play Award. In 2010 *Ghost Boy* (Keith Saha) won the Brian Way Award for the UK's Best New Play for Young People and Best Touring Production from the Liverpool Daily Post Awards. *Blackberry Trout Face* (Lawrence Wilson) received the 2010 Brian Way Award for UK's Best New Play for Young People and was short-listed as Best New Play by the Manchester Evening News 2009.

www.20storieshigh.org.uk

Signposts

Stop Hate

Working to challenge all forms of hate crime and discrimination through training, education and a reporting service

www.stophateuk.org / 0800 138 1625

Refugee Action

Providing support to people who've fled persecution, violence and harassment

www.refugee-action.org.uk / 0808 8000 630

Childline

Childline is a free UK confidential helpline dedicated to supporting vulnerable children and young people

www.childline.org.uk / 0800 1111

Young Minds

Emotional well-being and mental health for children and young people

www.youngminds.org.uk / 0808 802 5544

NSPCC

NSPCC helps children who've been abused to rebuild their lives. If you're worried about a child, contact their professional counsellors 24/7 for help, advice and support

www.nspcc.org.uk / 0808 800 5000

Barnardo's

Working with the most vulnerable young people across the UK, offering support services, campaigning and research expertise

www.barnados.org.uk / 0208 550 8822

Black

About *Black*

Black is a hard play to watch or read; it was also a hard play to write. Centred around sixteen-year-old Nikki, it explores her casual racism and the more extreme racism she encounters within the community she lives in. And it doesn't pull any punches. But it was a play I needed to write.

As a British Asian, I have been on the receiving end of racial abuse for as long as I can remember: sometimes casual and open, sometimes hidden, and other times at the end of violence. It was most acute for me, however, during my childhood and teenage years in the 1970s and 1980s, and as I grew older I naively thought that as a society we were evolving – things were moving on and getting better.

In 2014 a friend of mine told me that an African family she was working with were being terrorised by a group of young people and adults on a predominantly white estate on the outskirts of Liverpool. I was shocked and saddened that this was still happening. And I wanted to find out how widespread it was.

I began by talking to a number of young people from 20 Stories High Youth Theatre to see if they recognised what was happening. Some were Black British and others came from various African countries to Liverpool at different points in their childhood. Without exception they had all experienced casual racism and also varying levels of violence including smashed windows, arson attacks, knife attacks. Further research taught me that violent racist attacks weren't *decreasing* but had been steadily *increasing* in the UK and all over Europe since 2001. Yet it was obvious that the mainstream media were failing it report it. This was my impetus to write *Black*.

But instead of writing about my own experiences and those of the young people who had been on the receiving end, I wanted to write about what it was like to be the person dishing it out and ultimately what made them tick.

Growing up, I lived in a predominately white area where casual racism and the use of the 'N'-word were the norm and the young people I spoke to told me there were areas where this still felt true today. I also saw many of the people I grew up with starting to challenge those views of their family and community members through their teenage years, as parts of their world started to open up and expand. So the character of Nikki was born.

The monologue was written and performed as part of a bigger group of monologues I had written called *Headz*. From the audience responses, we felt that *Black* was the one that stood out as a play that should be given a fuller life. But I was aware that this was a very challenging play to watch and the audience had to sit through at least twenty minutes of hearing Nikki's prejudiced views before we started to see any shift.

So we began to develop the character of Precious by working with Q. Shanda, aka Chunky, a grime artist and DJ originally from Zimbabwe. His contributions were invaluable and we began to give Precious a voice. He told us of his own experiences and perspectives and also added a connection between the two characters that was much needed.

We have toured this play to theatre venues as well as community spaces, and every time the audience is usually split: there are those who are shocked that this level of racism still exists in the UK today and those who are painfully aware of it. This play was written before the Brexit referendum and the election of Trump, and with increased levels of racially-motivated violence, *Black* now feels even more urgent than it did in 2015.

For any young people wanting to perform extracts, or the play as a whole, I would really ask them to carefully consider the context and the audience and to have a real sensitivity to the issues it raises. In order to give some balance and to help audiences feel safe, it should never be performed publicly as Nikki's monologue without the character of Precious.

These are difficult times we are living in but, as in the play, if we keep including each other and talking to each other, then there is a way we can find the hope.

Keith Saha

Black was first performed in 2015 and toured to a range of theatre venues and community spaces. The original cast and creative team were:

Nikki   Abby Melia
Precious   Shanda

Director   Julia Samuels
Writer and Musical Director   Keith Saha
Additional Music Selection and Lyrics   Shanda
Dramaturg   Philip Osment

Designer   Miriam Nabarro
Lighting Designer   Douglas Kuhrt
Photographic Set Elements   Wesley Storey
Company Stage Manager   Ange John
Technical Assistant Stage Manager   Megan Sheeran
Schools and Communities Assistant Stage Manager
   Owen Jones
Production Manager and Set Construction
   Sam Kent, Lobster Productions

Big thanks to

John Au and all at the Anthony Walker Foundation, Raven Maguire, Anita Welsh, Bryony Doyle and all our Young Actors Company. Lina Sebuyange, Wesley Storey, Sarah Meath, Paul Williams, Xenia Bayer and all at the Liverpool Everyman Playhouse, Matthew Xia, Contacting the World, Clementinah Rooke.

Characters

Nikki, *female, sixteen, white, British*

Precious, *male, eighteen, Black, Zimbabwean*

Note on Staging

The play has been written to be performed with full, minimal or no set. All that is needed are chairs and basic props to make up the different locations of living room, bedrooms, bus stop, nursery and pub.

Note on Dialogue

When Nikki's dialogue includes quotation marks, she is reporting the words of other people in her story.

Scene One

A cul-de-sac on a housing estate on the outskirts of Liverpool.

Spring 2017, Monday morning.

As the audience enter, **Precious** *stands in the corner of the stage. He is mixing records behind a set of decks and a laptop. He has a mic. He plays heavy but bouncy grime tracks.*

As **Nikki** *enters, he changes the music to a country and western song, 'Ruby' by Kenny Rogers.*

They are in separate spaces.

Nikki *enters her living room. She gathers up her things for the day, putting them in her bag: purse, hairbrush, phone, cigarettes, lighter, make-up bag etc. She ties her hair back.*

She gets her phone out to call a taxi.

Nikki   Can I have a taxi please . . . ?
23 Maple Close.
Nik Naks nursery.

She looks out of the window. She speaks to the audience.

It was the dog that noticed them first . . .
This morning at breakfast.
Doesn't miss a trick . . . that one.
She jumps on the back of the sofa and starts barking out
    the window.
And we think she must have seen next door's cat or something
But she doesn't stop barking.
So I go over to the window to see what the fuss is . . .
And . . .
You'll never guess what she's barking at?
A coloured family . . .
Moving in over the close . . .
Blacks.

She struggles to fully project the word 'Blacks' as if it might offend, and instead mouths the word and half vocalises it.

And when I say black . . . I mean like *proper* black
Not like *Beyoncé* black
Like proper like . . . *African* black.

And me dad nearly spits his Shreddies out!
'Are you fucking kidding me . . . ?'
And the dog looks like she's gonna explode.
'Camilla, shut the fuck up . . . !'
But she doesn't stop.
And me dad looks like he's gonna have an heart attack!

I don't know why, but she's always barked at coloured people . . .
I remember when she was a pup, we took her on to Formby
    beach and there was this coloured family having a picnic.
And she just ran straight up to them . . . and started barking . . .
She wouldn't shut up!

We had to drag her away.
Ha! You should have seen the looks on their faces!
I shouldn't laugh really.

I don't know how we're gonna cope with them here now
    though.

Me mum's had to put her in the back yard to shut her up
    which pissed me dad off even more . . .
Cos (as soon she's outside) she shits everywhere . . .
and he hates shit.

When he takes her out . . .
he can't even pick it up . . .
He's a bit old-fashioned like that, me dad.
He says it should just go back into the earth as nature intended,
    so he always takes her on the back field, by the swings.

So, anyway we was all stood there at the window . . . gawping . . .
    curtain twitching, me nan calls it . . .
And you can see the rest of the close are doing it as well . . .
And some of the kids from over the road come out,
    sitting on their bikes . . .
Watching.

There was the dad . . . well, I think he was the dad, he could
    have been the granddad . . .
He was a bit on the grey side.
Then there was the mum, who was wearing some sort of
    tribal headgear.
And they just kept on coming . . .
Next up were two little sprogs . . .
I reckon they were twins by the look of them.
Must have been about two or three . . .
And then this lad steps out behind them . . . carrying a cage
    with a white rabbit in it!

Christ Almighty!
You should have seen the size of him!
Six foot something, skinny as a bean pole, all cap and *low
    down batty* jeans.
Arse hanging out thinking he was the mutt's nuts
Nosey bitch
    like he thought he was *Snoop Dogg* or something.
Although I've never heard of gangstas walking around the
    hood with rabbits under their arms . . .
Not the last time I looked, anyway.

And when l saw him . . .
I don't know why . . .
I could just feel it.
When he walked from the van to the house
All gangly-legged
And full of swagger.

I thought . . .
You're not gonna last five minutes round here.
I mean, all the lads round here wear North Face
    or if not that at least normal black trackies . . .
Not a bright red-and-gold Adidas or whatever it was . . .
I mean he's just asking for it . . . isn't he?

And the next thing you know, old Joan from over the road
    comes out.
So, me and me mum go and stand on the front step.

And Joan starts walking over to the mum with the head scarf,
    and the mum looks dead made-up to see her.
Looks like she thought she was gonna give her a moving-in
    present like she thought she was gonna give her a cake
    or something, the way she was grinning.
And she puts her hand out to Joan . . . you know like to shake it.
And the next thing you know, Joan's screaming and shouting
'GO HOME! YOU'RE NOT WANTED ROUND HERE!'
And these girls started filming it all on their phones
I bet it's on YouTube already.
'Go back to where you come from, cos we don't want any
    more trouble round here.'
She didn't even have her teeth in . . . It was hilarious . . .
And the coloured woman just put her hand up in Joan's face,
    she was having none of it, but then the husband come over
    and I reckon he was about to have a go . . .
When this stone comes from out of nowhere . . .
Right over Joan's head.
It wasn't a big stone mind,
wasn't like a brick or anything,
but the front window just shattered, glass everywhere
And Joan was like . . .
'SEE?! See what did I tell you?
There's gonna be murder round here . . .
There's gonna be murder.'

Then she turned on some of the lads . . .
'What are youse looking at? You cheeky little bastards . . . ?
I know who youse are, you're all animals!
You're ANIMALS!'
And they just scattered.

Then the coloured woman and the old fella bundled the
    kiddies up and took them in the house
And the lanky coloured lad . . . he was just stood in the middle
    of the street with the rabbit . . .
And he just looked at me . . .
Well, I don't know what he expected *me* to do . . .

She puts her coat on and grabs her bag.

The thing is, with all this drama going on, it's made me late
    for me first day at the nursery.
I'll probably get bollocked when I get in.
Where's me taxi?

She checks her phone.

I said to Mr Brookdale . . .
I said to him . . .
'There is no way I'm doing my work placement in a nursery!'
I hate kids . . . they knock me sick.
They're all snot and dribble and shitty nappies.
I was meant to do me placement at the Leisure Centre
    but it shut down before Christmas.

Everything's shutting down round here.
The pubs.
The shops.
The libraries.
Me dad says it's all *their* fault.
The immigrants.
We'll all be living under sharia law next.

Nikki *receives a text on her phone (from the taxi company), grabs her
bag and exits through her front door.*

Scene Two

Precious *cues up and plays the next track, a hardcore grime
instrumental with a heavy rumbling bass – full volume. Unaware of an
audience, he grabs the mic and spits his verse passionately.*

As the music plays, **Nikki** *resets the space as her bedroom. She sits on
the floor, reading messages on her phone.*

Precious   Waste man!

Should go replace man's thinking.
'Fraid that you're frightened of a *Zim King*

Dark in your heart,
Try make dark skin the victim.

Actions speak louder than words,
So now I'm listening.
Too many cowards in this thing.

Keep chatting your shit,
I hope your ring sting.

I said, Nobhead!
Look at your life, are you proud of it?

Living in a shroud o' shit,
No idea what power is.

Said that you're lucky that your face never
Found a fist.

Mr Nobhead!
Scared of an ethnic truth?

Take your jobs, your land,
And your lady too.

Thought you had me
when your pebbles came wading through.

I've got a message from Pressure to you . . .
Fuck you!

Scene Three

As the music fades, **Nikki** *drags herself up off the floor and goes to lie on her bed. It is late evening. She speaks to the audience.*

Nikki
I just heard them thumping up the stairs to bed.
I'm not going down though.
Not yet.
Just in case they come down and start having another go
I'll wait till I can hear him snoring . . .

I'm starving . . . and all.
I haven't even had me tea yet.
They've probably given it to Camilla.

I can be a stubborn bitch me, when I want to.

I know he only means well.
But . . . I'm sixteen . . . for frig's sake.

Marie from next door come round to see if *everything was alright.*
Nosey bitch.
She knows exactly what was going on, cos you can hear
    everything through these walls.
She always comes sniffin' round after me dad's been on one.

She looks at her phone again.

None of this would have happened anyway if *they* hadn't
    have turned up today.
The coloured twins . . .
at the nursery.

I couldn't believe it when I seen them skipping up the path.
I thought 'Oh God here comes trouble . . .
The last thing we need is stones flying through the nursery
    windows.'
Can you imagine?

They settled in alright though,
    started playing . . . and mixing in well, like.
The other kids didn't bat an eyelid . . .

I thought . . . just give that a few years!

It's funny though.
Nik Naks.
Not what I expected.
The boss Marge is a bit of snotty bitch . . . but Janice is sound . . .
She's one of the workers.
Showed me where I could go for a sly ciggy at dinner time . . .
Cos you're not supposed to smoke in front of the kids.
It's not as bad as I thought it was gonna be.
Better than school . . . anyway.

Apart from the stink.

Janice says you get used to it after a while
and we should be grateful cos it's not as bad as old people's
shite,
and she used to work in an old people's home . . . so she
should know.

So after we had juice and biscuits . . . *she* comes over to me . . .
You know . . . the little coloured girl?
Jillian her name is, but you don't say it with a 'juh', you say
it with a 'guh', so it's
Gillian apparently!

*Jillian is pronounced with a soft J-sound, and Gillian is pronounced
with a hard G-sound.*

Anyway so, she starts giving me all this stuff . . . from the
pretend shop . . .
you know like those little . . . miniature packets of pretend
food you get . . .
And she wouldn't stop . . .
A little packet of cornflakes . . . then a little tin of beans . . .
and a little carton of milk.
I couldn't get rid of her.
And I don't know if it was cos she recognised me from the
close . . .
But she just wouldn't stop following me around.

'You've got a friend for life there . . . ' Janice says . . .

And then to top it all off she comes waddling up to me with
a *book*.
The Cat in the Hat.
And I'm like . . . 'There is no way on God's earth . . . I am
reading that!'
And Janice is like 'Go on . . . '

And I feel ashamed cos I never read out aloud.
Ever.
I hate it . . .

In English, when they make us . . . when they go round the
   class . . . I always find an excuse, go the bog or something . . .
   Or pretend I've got a sore throat.
But Janice is looking at me,
So I think, fuck it!

So I go and sit in the corner by the window, away from
   everyone,
so no one can hear me
And sure enough she follows me over and plonks herself in
   me lap.
And I'm reading it to her dead quiet . . . you know . . . just
   so she can hear me.
And she starts giggling away
Cos it's actually funny . . .
It's a funny book.
I was surprised.
Cos the film's shite, innit?
Seen it on Netflix at our Mark's
with that Jim Carrey . . . ?!
Well, he's just annoying isn't he?
Ruins it!

Anyway.
And, as I'm reading it,
   she's chuckling away
And I don't mean to be sly or anything . . .
but . . .
she . . . smelt . . . funny!
As I'm reading it I get this whiff . . .
   and she just smelt different from all the other kids . . .
And I don't know what it was . . .
It was like . . .
It was like some sort of *food* . . .
   but not like some Pakistani kids might smell of curry.
It was like a sweet smell . . .
Like coconut . . .
It was probably something in her hair . . .
Cos she's got these dead tight little plaits.

Anyway she's laughing away
And her little brother Vivian comes over . . . to see what all
    the fuss is about
and then one by one nearly all the other kids
    start waddling over and plonking their little arses on the
    mat in front of me.
It was hilarious . . . !
It was like feeding the ducks in the park with me granddad.
And Janice was just grinning at me and gave me a big thumbs up.

And I thought look at *me*! Mary fucking Poppins!

In the afternoon . . . we shoved them all in front of *Monsters Inc.*
While some of us went in the back yard for a ciggy.

Janice said they're all going the karaoke at The Feathers on
    Friday night and I can go with them if I want.
I said 'Oh, The Feathers that's near ours that . . . ! Me dad
    drinks in there sometimes . . . Big Mick . . . do you know
    him?'
She said she didn't know him, but she knows *of* him, like.
Everyone knows me dad round ours . . . he's like a local
    celebrity.
You know, cos of all the charity work he's done and stuff . . .
Did a run for the local hospice and that . . .
    after me Nan got cancer.

I said I'd ask me mum about the karaoke,
But I'll have to wait until I'm speaking to them again . . .

Janice said she's gonna do Lady Gaga, which should be a laugh.
I don't know what I'm gonna do yet.
I think I'll either do 'Girls Just Wanna Have Fun' or something
    by Taylor Swift.

The last time I did karaoke was at our Carla's wedding.
Marry-oke they called it, it was boss!
Me dad made a show of us though . . . kept on hogging the
    mic with his Kenny-Rogers-country-and-western-shite . . .
    or whatever it was!

So I was amazingly having an alright day.
But then at home time
I was putting me coat on,
Getting ready to go home . . .
And you'll never guess who comes strolling up the path?
It was only Kanye-bloody-West, coming to pick up the twins.

He spotted me straight away . . . came over to introduce himself.
And he was dead polite and formal, like.
Wanted to shake me hand and everything . . .
He put me on edge.

He said he'd seen me on the close and that his name was
    Precious.
I said 'Precious? I thought that was a girl's name.'
He said it could be both.

I reckon he must have been dead posh where he comes from
    in Africa.
I don't know why . . . he just had something about him.
He was dead sure of himself.
Cocky like.

Then the twins just shot straight up to him
And we sort of started walking out together . . . It was by
    accident really.
But I didn't want to . . .
I didn't wanna be seen dead with them.
Can you imagine?
So I pretended I'd left me phone inside and said ta-ra.

When I went back in, Janice had been clocking us.
'You've got an admirer there! Eh?! Young Mo Farah? Very
    dashing!'
I said 'Don't talk soft!'
And I could feel meself going red . . .
I can see why some girls might fancy him . . .
I mean, he is good-looking and that
But he's not my *type* if you know what I mean.
Besides, I've been seeing Donno since I was thirteen.

And I must have waited about what?
A good ten minutes.
But when I went out, they were still there playing on the
    grass on the front.
He said he'd been waiting for me . . . so we could catch the
    bus home together,
And I was just like . . .
'Errrrrr . . . yeah . . . sound . . . whatever!'

But on the way to the bus stop
I don't know why . . .
I just panicked . . .
And I could feel people starting to look at us.
I mean, can you imagine *me* being seen on the bus with *them*?
Well, people might get the wrong idea . . .
So I said . . .
'I'll tell you what mate . . . Why don't I show you a different
    way home? Over the back field . . . it only takes about
    twenty minutes . . . '
I hate walking as well me, . . . I'm a lazy cow.
So anyway, as we was walking back
He was telling me all about how his family had come
    from Zimbabwe when he was ten, then they went to live in
    Stockport, and now his mum had got a job in Liverpool . . .
    and blah blah blah . . . blah blah blah.
On and on . . . He was boring me shitless
Like I was his new bezzie mate!

And then eventually, we got to the point where we had to
    join the main road,
You know, . . . just before the Tesco Extra.
And Jillian, sorry *Gillian*, decides she wants to get out the
    buggy and hold me hand.
And the next thing you know, the lad – *Precious* – has got hold
    of the other one.
And she's shouting 'Swing! Swing! Give me a swing!'
And people are starting to look.
And I feel ashamed.

And the little lad Vivian's screaming to get out of the buggy,
　　cos he wants a frigging swing.
And then I just see this van coming towards us . . . hundred
　　miles an hour . . .
Brakes right in front of us.
Skids onto the pavement.
And then *he* gets out,
Grabs me by the arm
　　and shoves me in the back of the van with all his nasty
　　decorating stuff
And I'm like . . . 'Dad! Gerroff me!'
And then he grabs Precious by the back of his head, whispers
　　something in his ear . . . gets in the van and drives off . . .
And I'm screaming at him . . .
'What did you do that for?'
And I could see out the back window, Precious just standing
　　there frozen,
With Vivian screaming in his buggy and Gillian just stood
　　there gobsmacked holding his hand . . .

Beat.

When we got back home.
That's when they both try to lay the law down
But I was having none of it.

Me mum said 'We don't want any bricks flying through our
　　window just cos you fancy a different flavour of meat.'
She's got a lovely way with words me mum.
And I'm like 'I don't even fancy him . . . why can't you get that
　　into your thick skulls?'

Then after all the screaming and shouting
　　me dad tries the softly softly approach . . .
Like he's one of those wildlife people off the telly, trying
　　to tame a wild animal.
He pulls his chair up next to me . . . and he's almost whispering
But I can tell he's not calm, cos I can see the veins twitching
　　on the side of his head.

'Listen . . . you know we both love you very much, don't make
    this hard for me . . .
Just keep your distance.'
And I'm like . . . 'How am I meant to keep me distance when
    they go to the same nursery as me?
And anyway, I didn't ask for them to follow me home.'
And he's like 'Okay, but if it happens again you call me up
    and I'll come and pick you up in the van
Do you understand?'

But I didn't say anything,
I just ran up here and shut me door.
I don't want them treating me like a kid.

Everyone's jangling about me now on *Insta*, apparently.
I'm fuming.
Little Dickheads calling me an *NL*.

I phoned Donno . . . left him loads of messages . . . but he's
    not getting back.
Prick!
I've had a few nice texts off me bezzies . . . Joanne and Abi . . .
    but –
Let's just say there are other mates out there who are keeping
    dead quiet . . .
Well, I thought they were me mates anyway.

Are people so really fucking bored around here . . .
that they have to just fucking latch on to any little piece of
    drama . . . ?
Anything that will spice up their own sad little fucking
    lives . . . ?

She goes to the window.

You should have seen it out there before!
There were loads of them, they were all out . . . Joan, Marie
    from next door, Jim who does Neighbourhood Watch with
    me dad, loads of the local kids.
Most of them have gone.
Still a few left though.

I saw me dad talking to them before . . .
On his way back from walking the dog.

Ha!
The state of him.
I had to laugh when I seen him, though.
I couldn't believe it.
He was carrying Camilla's shit in a bag!
He looked hysterical.
I mean . . . It just didn't look like *him*.

Nikki *stews.*

It just goes to show how much he cares I suppose . . .
How much he wants things to better around here.

People sometimes get the wrong impression about me dad . . .
It does me head in.
In town on a Saturday
I can just see people like . . . proper staring . . .
Proper staring.
Just because he's big and bald and fat and tattooed and kicks
    off every now and then . . .
It doesn't mean he's a −
(*Correcting herself.*) It doesn'ts mean he's a thug.

Some people call him a racist
    but he's not . . .
He just speaks the truth.

You're not allowed to say anything any more
I always get shot down at school by the teachers if I try to
    say anything about Muslims or Pakistani paedophile
    gangs . . . or attacks on our soldiers.

My Uncle Drew . . . well, his lad . . . Kyle, who's my cousin,
    he was in the army . . . for years . . . went everywhere . . .
    Northern Ireland, Iraq, Afghanistan; you name it, he
    went there . . . ,
Spent years fighting for *our* country.

And I don't know what happened exactly,
    but in the end . . . he had to pack it all in for health reasons
    or something . . .
He was only nineteen or twenty . . .
but when he comes out he couldn't even get a proper place
    to live . . .
He ended up in a hostel in town.
A friggin' hostel! Can you believe that?
And then you get the likes of *them* coming over . . .
They click their fingers and they get a house, just like that.

It's because he cares . . .
He cares so much about this country and what's happening
    to it . . .
And when people start coming over and taking our jobs and
    our houses and everything.
It's just –
It just gets –
It's too much for him.
And I know he doesn't always go about things the right way . . .
But . . .

In the morning . . .
I'm gonna go downstairs give him a big hug,
Tell him I'm sorry.
And tell him that I'm not gonna go anywhere near them . . .
And I'm gonna keep me distance.
And I know they haven't done anything wrong,
But . . .
It's not worth the hassle.
I mean there are plenty of other workers there, who can read
    Cat in the Hat to them isn't there?
Why does it have to be me?

Music.

Scene Four

Precious *is playing a slow, haunting trip-hop beat. He grabs the mic and addresses the audience for the first time.*

Precious   Once upon a grime in England's green and
    pleasant land

A young princess was locked in a tower by her father
The evil king – painter, decorator.
The king stayed awake
Day and night . . .
And
Night and day . . .

He watched the rising of the moon
And the falling of the sun,

All to protect his daughter
From the clutches of . . .
The Black Beast

The monster from the caves
That lurked in the shadows
The Black Beast.
Who had come to pollute his land
And corrupt his daughter
With his evil seed.

But so fearful of the beast was the king,
So blinded by rage,
That he didn't realise . . .
he was killing the very thing he was trying to protect.

And so with a sword in one hand and a paintbrush in the other,
He vowed to get rid of the beast and his beastly kind by
    any means necessary . . .

But as the beast looked out from his cave . . .
Protected from the king's army by his boxes of vinyl,
and slow melodic bass

He remembered what his own father had taught him when
     they once fled violence. To stay calm, and to not take up
     arms.
He did not want no beef.

He did not want to go to war.
He just wanted the world . . .
To fall in love . . .
With . . .
Dub.

The beat suddenly stops and **Precious** *switches the music up and plays
a slow, melodic dub beat. In the distance, we hear the sound of traffic.*

Scene Five

Late afternoon. **Nikki** *stands at a bus stop on a deserted junction.*

Nikki   All afternoon, I've had it going round and round
     in me head what I was gonna say to him.
I had it all planned out
I was gonna say . . .
'Sorry mate . . . I know you've been through a rough time, but
     I can't walk home with youse today cos there's just too
     much going on. Don't take it personally like . . . '
But I couldn't . . .
When he asked me to go with him . . .
I just put me coat on and ran out the door . . .
I phoned me dad to pick me up like he said, but he didn't
     answer.

I just hope the bus comes before they catch up with me.
God! I feel like a right bitch now

The police came into Nik Nak's today,
     had a word with bitch-face-boss-woman
Then they called me into the office.
Well, I nearly shat meself . . .

Well, you do, don't you, when the bizzies are around? Even if
    you haven't done anything wrong . . .
All I could think about was that iPhone I bought off that
    woman from the pub at Christmas . . .
But it wasn't me they were looking for.
They were looking for Precious.
I said 'What you asking me for? I hardly know the lad . . .
Although I'm not surprised you're after him . . . what is it,
    drugs?'

They said there'd been an incident this morning on the close.
Apparently a gang of lads, about six of them, broke into
    their house . . .
Trashed the place, and smeared shit all over the walls
And then one of them took the rabbit out of the hutch
    and hung it over the front door with one of the kids'
    skipping ropes.
The thing was though, as they were tying it up . . . the mum
    come home.
Caught them doing . . . tried to stop them.
And then . . .
Then they battered her.
She's in intensive care.

I said 'Well I do know him a bit . . . he goes to the Community
    College in town . . .
And he's doing business studies.
You could try him there?'

They said to carry on as normal with the twins
    and not to say a word until a relative comes to pick them up
    at the end of the afternoon.
Then they went . . .

After dinner time, Gillian came up to me holding the *Cat in
    the Hat* book
She said to me –
She said . . . 'Are you not my friend?'
I said 'Of course I'm your friend . . . what makes you think
    that?'

And she just give me a little shrug.

She could tell I'd been avoiding her . . .
Well, they're not soft are they, kids?
They get on to everything, don't they?
And I'm like
'Why don't you go and play in the Wendy house with Chloe
    and Jamie?'
But she was having none of it . . .
She just plonked herself down on the mat in front of me . . .

And I know I shouldn't have done it
But I couldn't help meself.
I picked her up and took her into the corner and I read to her.
The Cat in the Hat
You should have seen her little face light up.
Big, brown chocolate eyes!
Look at me, she's turning me fucking soft!

Later in the afternoon *he* turns up. Precious with a social
    worker or someone . . .
And they take the twins into the back office to . . . you
    know . . .
To tell them what's been going on
And then next thing you know, bitch-face-boss-woman
    asks Janice to ask me if I can go into there with them . . .
    you know for *moral support* or whatever.
And I was like . . . 'Do I have to?
I'm no good at that sort of thing.'
And she was like, 'Go on, they relate to you!'

But I didn't do anything really . . . I just had Gillian on me lap
    and he had Vivian.

They told them that their mum had taken poorly and had to
    go into hossy for a bit and . . . and she'd be back soon when
    she was better
I could tell he'd been crying . . . his eyes were all red.
Apparently he said Joan had been helping him clear the place up.
I said . . . 'Are you serious? Joan-over-the-road-Joan?'

He said, 'It was disgusting . . . there was shit everywhere.'

He said the police thought it was only dog shit . . . not
     human cos they'd left a plassy bag of it on the front with half
     of it left in.
As if they thought dog shit isn't as bad as human?

When they were getting ready to leave
I had a quiet word with the social worker . . . I said to her . . .
     'You can't send them back to that house . . . can't you put
     them in a B and B somewhere?' She said Precious and the
     dad had refused.
She said there would be some sort of protection for them . . .
You know police checking in on them . . . for a few nights
     until it had all cleared over.
I said 'That's good! I hope they catch the little bastards.'
She said the bizzies had been doing door-to-door enquiries
     asking for witnesses to come forward
     but nobody had seen anything apparently.
The only descriptions they've got to go on is six white lads
     all aged between sixteen and nineteen.
Brown hair, all wearing black trackies.

And then he came up to me with the twins all zipped and
     buttoned up waiting to go home . . .
And he said would I walk him home?
And I just ran out the door . . .
What a dickhead . . . !

Nikki *sees people in the distance. She squints.*

Shit . . . is that them?
I can see three little black dots in the distance
I swear to God I need glasses . . .
Oh . . . they're going the backfield way . . .

She shouts.

Precious! . . . Precious?! Wait for us! I'll come with yers!

She walks off purposefully towards them. **Precious** *cues up and plays
the next track – it is Miriam Makeba's 'Qhude'.*

Scene Six

Early evening. As the music plays, **Precious** *comes out from behind his decks.*

He and **Nikki** *see each other for the first time. He welcomes her into his home and takes her coat and bag.*

He offers her a seat and then leaves her to make a phone call.

Nikki *is left by herself, lost in her own thoughts.*

The music continues. **Precious** *talks down the microphone like it's a mobile phone.*

He speaks in his mother tongue Ndebele. (Translations in brackets.)

Precious   Yebo mama.
[*Hi Mum.*]

Mama, yimi, uPrecious.
[*Mum, it's me, Precious.*]

Ngifona ukuthi ngizwe ukuthi uzva njani.
[*I'm just ringing to see if you're okay.*]

Kuhle.
[*Good.*]

Baphilile, akukho okubi.
[*They're okay, they're safe.*]

Balele.
[*They're sleeping.*]

Ngikuphatheleni?
[*Do you want me to bring you anything?*]

Imagazini yakhoke? Ngingabuya layo nxa ufuna, kumbe ibhuku.
[*What about your magazine? I can bring that if you want, or a book.*]

Kulungile.
[*Okay.*]

Ngizabuya ngizokubona kusasa.
[*Well, I'll come and visit tomorrow.*]

Ngiyakuthanda lawe Mama.
[*Love you too, Mum.*]

Ngizakwenza njalo . . . Bhayibhayi, Mama.
[*I will . . . bye, Mum.*]

Bhayibhayi
[*Bye.*]

He hangs up and sits down. Music fades.

Scene Seven

Late evening. **Nikki** *is now alone in* **Precious**' *bedroom. She stares out of the window.*

Nikki   The living room lights have just gone off.
He's gone upstairs now . . .
I can see him in the bedroom window, staring at me.
He's fuming.
I tried to go round to get me clothes . . .
But he's bolted and deadlocked all the doors.
I can't even use me key.

Me mum's gonna meet me in the Tesco's café tomorrow
     morning before work, to give me a change of clothes
     and that.
I texted her back saying . . . 'Why can't you just bring them
     over?
I'm only over the road for Christ's sake!
It's not like you're not gonna catch *Ebola* or anything!'
At least the smell of shit's gone now . . . well nearly.
Marie brought some joss sticks over before . . . which was nice.

After I put the twins to bed
The community police officer woman come round
Said it was good that someone was here to support them.
I said 'I'll stay for as long as they need me, as long as I'm
     useful . . . It's the least I can do . . . you know considering.'

She said 'What do you mean considering?'
I said . . . 'Well . . . no one else is helping out.'
Then the cheeky bitch started accusing *me*.
She said 'Are you *sure* you don't know anything . . . or anybody
    that might be involved? . . . you can tell us in strictest
    confidence . . . '
I said . . . 'You're the police! You're meant to know who the
    criminals are around here. Did you ever even catch the
    people that petrol bombed the Paki shop last summer?'
Precious shot me a look . . .
She said 'No . . . the incident at the "Asian" shop was still
    under investigation.'
Then she went . . .
Useless bag of shite.

Someone else is coming round to check in on us later.
The twins are oblivious to all what's going on . . .
Apart from the rabbit . . .
They noticed it straight away.
Precious told them that it had gone on holiday to Stockport
    to see his cousin
Rabbit Clive at the pet shop.

It was weird . . . cos I thought they'd miss their mum more
    but they didn't seem to . . . well, they haven't shown it if
    they do.
They were just dead excited that I was staying over . . .
You know . . . having a *sleepover*!
I read to them . . . at bedtime . . . They went out like lights.

Precious is keeping watch by the downstairs window . . .
While I'm meant to be getting some sleep . . .
As if I can sleep with all this going on!
We're gonna do it in shifts . . .
While his dad's at the 'ozzy.[1]

It was a bit awkward after the twins went to bed . . .

---

1. *ozzy*: slang for hospital.

He wasn't in a very talkative mood.
And I didn't really know what to say to him.

So we just watched Gogglebox.

She looks out of the window, to check what's happening.

I can't believe there's still kids outside now.
No one dare do anything now anyway.
Not while I'm here.

And he might not be talking to me . . .
But I know he's . . . watching
Over the road . . .
Any sign of trouble . . . he'll be over like a shot.

Well . . .
I hope so anyway.

Me mum said it'll take a few days for him to come round.
She said 'You shouldn't have flaunted it in his face, it was like
    a red rag to a bull.'
And part of me knows she's right . . . cos I know what he's
    like . . .
But it's no excuse for what he did . . .

After I caught up with them.
I said sorry – for running off, like.
And we started walking home together, over the backfield.
Gillian and Vivian were running around being hyper as usual.
Precious' head was just a proper mess with all what was
    going on . . .
And in me head . . . like what I was gonna do . . .
    was walk with them until we got near ours . . .
    and then I'd make me excuses and nip into the shop or
    something . . . and let them walk the last bit by
    themselves . . .
You know, so I wouldn't get into trouble with me dad.
But I couldn't.
So I just kept walking.
And I'm glad I did.

Cos by the time we got to our close . . . it was swarming
   with little dickheads who had come for a nose . . .
Someone had Snapchatted the picture of the dead rabbit,
And there was loads of vile stuff being said . . . about hanging
   and who was gonna be next . . .
'Kill the black bastards.'
and stuff like that . . .
But worse.
I don't even wanna say it . . .

And everything just sort of happened at the same time.

Hannah Byron and her skanky mate Jodie Jones was sat on
   the wall filming us and then there were these little pricks
   on their bikes who just started like circling us,
And spitting on the ground.
Not spitting *at* us mind, just on the road . . .
Like inches from our feet . . .
you know, trying to get a reaction.

And then Joan comes out and starts shouting at them.
You know . . . telling them to leave us alone.
And Precious started to strap the twins in the buggy.

And the next thing I hear is my dad from our front step shouting,
'Nikki, get your arse in here now!'
And as I turned round to him . . .

One of the lads . . . I'm not sure . . .
But I think it was the ginger one,
It could have been the other one,
But one of them muttered under his breath
Nigger lover
And as soon as he said that I just lost it.
BAM!
I took the ginger prick out,
Got him straight in his jaw.
I could hear the crack as it knocked him off his bike.

The twins looked terrified of me . . . so did Precious, now
   that I think about it.

And then all the other kids started legging it over,
Screaming and laughing.
They missed out on the dead rabbit show before, so now
    they wanted another.

And I was like,
'Come on then . . . does anyone one else wanna go?'
And I could hear me dad coming over . . .
'Nikki! Get in the house NOW!'

And I was like, 'Precious, just get them inside will you?!'
And he ran in with them . . .

The lad had got up off the floor by now . . . and all his mates
    were laughing at him.
'Anyone wanna call me that again? Go on! Just try it!
I'll fucking knock youse all out . . . you fucking gimps!'
And Joan was stood there, clapping me!
And Marie come out and was trying to calm me down.

But the next thing I knew . . .
me dad grabbed me by the back of the neck and tried
    to like . . .
frog march me into the house . . .
just like he used to, when I was six
But harder.
And I'm like 'Get off me, I'm not a kid!'
Then he just threw me on our front step.

And all the lads and some of the girls were cheering . . .
    making monkey noises.

'It's them you should be having a go at, not me! '
But he was having none of it.
'They called me a nigger lover!'
And then . . .
He bent down and he whispered in me ear
'You are a nigger lover! Now get in the house!'
And I just froze . . .
And then me mum come running down the stairs.
And she was like

'Get yourself in the house and stop making a show!'

But I couldn't . . .

I couldn't go in.
So . . . I just picked meself up off our step
    and started walking . . .
Straight across the road,
Past the dickheads,
Past the skanky bitches with their phones,
Past Marie,
Past Joan,
And knocked on Precious' door.

So here I am.
On the other side.

She goes back to the window.
I just wish they'd all go home.
I know nothing's gonna happen . . . I just wanna go to sleep.
But I can't.
Cos there's one thing that's really bugging me . . .
I can't get that image out of me head of me dad picking up
    Camilla's shit in a plassy bag the other night!

He was out with her about an hour ago . . .
And he wasn't carrying any bag then.

Besides the descriptions was all of young lads . . .
I'm just being stupid.
I best get me head down . . .

Precious said the twins always wake up at six in the morning
    and they'll probably want to come in and jump on me.
I said 'They better frigging not!
I don't want any cheeky little monkeys jumping all over me
    first thing . . . '
I'm not a morning person!

She sits on the bed and takes her shoes off.

Scene Eight

Precious *plays an upbeat melodic African hip-hop beat.* **Precious**
grabs the mic as **Nikki** *starts setting up the nursery. He addresses the
audience.*

Precious   Okay children . . .
Are you sitting comfortably?
Then I'll begin.
Let me hear you make some noise for DJ Pressure.

Sound effect of children chanting 'Yay!'

So the Cat in the Hat
Has gone *away*
And Mary Poppins is here to *stay*
As I keep nightwatch in the *bay*
I hope no more dead rabbits come our way
I've found another game that we can *play*
Let's find words that with rhyme with '*Yay*'

Sound effect of children chanting 'Yay!'

Like *decay.*

Sound effect of children chanting 'Yay!'

So every *day*
My heart turns to *clay*
As I pray night and *day*
That my dear mum will be *okay*
I call up to God but as I *pray*
My heart starts to *stray*
Back to Zim-bab-*we*

Sound effect of children chanting 'Yay!'

Back to Zim-bab-*we*
The heat of Sun
Feels far far *away*
I look out my window
And all I see is *grey*

The boys with the bricks
See me as their *prey*

Sound effect of children chanting 'Yay!'

Just another black *cliché*?
Another low down batty wearing
Snap Back Black *cliché*

Another black *cliché*?
Another low-down batty wearing
Snap back black *cliché*

So when I say *pray*
you say *yay*
Pray

Sound effect of children chanting 'Yay!'

So when I say *pray*
you say *yay*
Pray

Sound effect of children chanting 'Yay!'

So when I say *pray*
you say *yay*
Pray

Sound effect of children chanting 'Yay!'

Music fades. **Precious** *sits down.*

Scene Nine

The following Friday, late afternoon.

Nikki *is tidying up the toys at Nik Naks nursery – we hear the children playing outside. She has her nursery pinny over her clothes.*

Nikki   Bitch-face said if I ever want to come back and
   work with them properly
   I have to finish me GCSEs, then do a childcare course.

I said I'll defo think about it, . . . so I might be applying to
    go to the community college in town.
Ha! Can you believe that? Me at college . . . ? Mr Brookdale
    nearly had a heart attack.

It's been a lovely last day though . . .
They give me a card and a box of Celebrations and everything!
I said 'I've only been here two weeks!'

Janice said that her and a few of the other girls want to take
    me to the karaoke at The Feathers tonight . . . you know
    as a sort of leaving do . . .
We never got to go last week . . .
You know, with all the carryings on.

I said I'd think about it . . .

Can you imagine me going in there with all the shite that's
    gone on?
It'd be a pure kick off!
And I don't want to ruin their night out.
If I do go . . . I'll have to warn me mum and tell her to tell
    me dad not to be there.

She looks wistfully around the nursery.

The past few days haven't been the same without them.
It's . . .
quieter . . .

They're at a new nursery now . . . in town.
I hope they're looking after them okay.
Cos Gillian gets grumpy if she doesn't have her mid-morning
    nap.

He said they were all moving into a hostel.
I said 'A hostel? They can't be putting the twins in a place
    like that.'
Especially if it's as nasty as the one our Kyle is in.
They need a proper house.
He said they had a look and it wasn't that bad . . .

And there was a house that been allocated for them . . .
    it just needed doing up first.

It's near the back of the cathedral in town . . .
You know, the old one?
So they'll be safe there . . . you know 'cos it's a bit more
    'mixed' apparently.

He said I can go and visit any time I wanted.
I was like . . . 'Yeah, defo, that'd be sound!'
But . . .
You say things, don't you?
Anyway, I'd feel ashamed going to that part of town.
Everyone'd be looking at me.

It's weird cos I got quite comfy there in the end . . . found
    me routine.
Helping Precious and his dad with the shopping and cleaning
    and the cooking . . .
Well, I say cooking, I can burn Pot Noodles me!
Me mum said to me once 'You can't boil an egg in a friggin'
    kettle.'
I said 'Why not? It's boiling water innit?!'
I could tell it was doing me mum's head in though, me being
    over there helping out, cos I've never lifted a finger at
    home . . . didn't even know how to use the washing machine.

His dad was dead nice though . . . dead quiet and gentle . . .
    Couldn't believe it when he put that country and western
    CD on though! I thought 'Friggin' 'ell it's just like being
    at ours!'

Well, at least we didn't get any more stones through the windows.
We did get more shit through the letterbox though.
And God knows how they did this, but a couple of days
    before they moved out
Someone had turned the water off.
Can you believe that?
I was giving Gillian a bath and turned the taps on and nothing.
And that was the last straw really . . .

The mum was ready to come out of 'ozzy and there was no
     way she could go back to that . . . so . . .
Off they went.

On the morning . . . when they moved out . . .
Me dad was sat out on the wall opposite with Camilla –
     gloating – arms folded,
Waiting for me to come home with me tail between me legs
But . . .
I just blanked him.
There's no way I'm going back home . . .
I can't even look at him.
Let alone talk to him.

Not after what he did.

I'm stopping at me mate Joanne's for a bit,
     till I figure out what to do.
Her mum said I can stay as long as I want . . . she's sound.
Said she went out with a mixed-race-lad-fella once and there
     was murder round here . . .
So she sort of knew what I was going through.
But I said to her,
'I didn't even fancy him though, that's where everyone got it
     wrong!
He might have fancied me, but who could blame him?'

It's me mum I feel sorry for . . .
Trying to be the go-between.

I said 'Of course I still love him . . .
He's me dad isn't he!?
He just needs to say sorry.
And he needs to change.'
She said 'Change?! Your dad? Change?!
He's too old for that . . . he's never gonna change.'
I said 'That's bollocks . . . I've changed . . .
Look . . . I don't say "Paki shop" any more, cos I know that
     offends some people.
I say Asian shop.'
And I don't say coloured I always say . . .

Black.

She continues to tidy the toys. As she does so, she picks up a book – The Cat in the Hat.

She sits down, opens up the book and reads a couple of pages out loud.

Precious *plays a mellow, instrumental track.*

Nikki *closes the book and puts the last box away.*

She takes one last look at the nursery.

Nikki *takes off her pinny and replaces it with a new top.*

Scene Ten

We hear the sound effect of ambient pub noise over the music.

Nikki *is going out. She puts in her earrings and does her hair.*

She arrives at The Feathers. It is karaoke night!

The music fades out – the pub ambience sound effect gets louder.

She grabs a drink, tentatively picks up a mic and looks out at the audience.

Nikki   Okay so . . . this one's for someone who is really special to me, but I don't see any more . . .

She nods to the karaoke host, behind the audience.

We hear 'Country Roads' by John Denver, karaoke version.

Nikki *sings. It is heartfelt determined and beautiful.*

On the second verse of the song, we hear **Precious** *in his bedroom, performing lyrics over a beat with the same tempo. The music merges.*

Precious   DJ pressure
Staying defiant
Not being compliant.
I'm strong
like a giant.
I'm not a subtraction
I'm additional.

You can't take me apart
I'm not divisional.

Knock me down?
Pressure, come bouncing back.
Back on the track
Like the Cat in the Hat

Now I've fixed my abode
Sky lights on the path that I travel down.
My country road
Our country now

He sings the 'Country Roads' chorus with her.

He then raps over her last verse.

I keep on building blocks
towards the heavens.
They keep crashing,
Like a hundred nine-elevens.

I'll keep playing this sound
until you hear it
Bass is my weapon
Though you shouldn't have to fear it

Sometimes I wish that I didn't exist,
But as long as I live the pressure is real.

For king, for country

I will stand up on my own
Sit up on my throne
And make this land my home.

Our country,
Our roads.
And make this land my home,

Our country

Our road.

Fade to black.

She's Leaving Home

About *She's Leaving Home*

She's Leaving Home is a play performed in a real house for an intimate audience.

2017 was the fiftieth anniversary of The Beatles' seminal album *Sgt. Pepper's Lonely Hearts Club Band.* As part of the celebrations, Liverpool Culture Company commissioned artists and companies to respond to a track on the album. 20 Stories High were given *She's Leaving Home.* It felt like a perfect choice for us and is one of my favourites.

There were some things that came to us straight away. We knew that we didn't want to make a piece that retold the original and well-documented story of the young woman who left home in 1967, but wanted to explore what *She's Leaving Home* meant to young adults in 2017. We also wanted to make a play in a real house in Liverpool 8 (or Toxteth as most people know it) and we wanted one of the young people that had come up through 20 Stories High Youth Theatre to be the young woman referred to in the title. We also wanted live music – a cellist who had a relationship to the haunting strings on the original track and also a rich visual world that evoked the original artwork of the cover.

We started off the process by inviting a group of young people from 20 Stories High Youth Theatre and Young Actors Company to a workshop led by Phelim McDermott from Improbable theatre company. Using the 'Worldwork' techniques – where a group of people investigate a topic through discussion and role play – we started off with the simple question 'What is home?'

After an intensive day, the narratives that resonated for the young adults in the room were miles away from the young woman in the original song. For many of them, leaving home wasn't an option, even though many of them desperately wanted to. This was mainly for financial/economic reasons, but also many of them were young carers who were looking after siblings, parents and other family members. Many were walking a tightrope of wanting to stay and support their families but also carrying the guilt of feeling trapped and wanting to leave.

So we had our main narrative thread. The next part of the process was finding a house and playing in it. After much searching we met with Liverpool 8 community activists Teresa MacDermott and Joe Farrag. and found the prefect place to realise the world Liverpool 8/Toxteth has a complex and political history in terms of housing and we wanted this to be a strong narrative thread.

We then also cast the fabulous Brodie Arthur an ex-Youth Theatre member and Liverpool 8 native who had strong resonances with story and also the community.

We then began to explore the actual house: all its creaks and sounds, the outside world, the front window, the noises from the stairs and upstairs, the sounds of the kids playing on the street and the cars passing by the front window. A whole new world of challenges and opportunities to make a show – and a million miles away from making one in a theatre space.

I then went away and started to write the monologue for Kelsey, while Phelim with Alison and Julia the director began to concentrate on the visual world, and created the ghost character of 1960s Woman and also the unseen character of Reece (played deftly by a stage manager).

The play was then performed in the house for fifteen performances to an audience of international festival-goers and residents of Liverpool 8. It then went on to a mini living-room tour of people's houses in the local area for an invited audience of friends and family. At the same time local community artists Curtis Watt and Nikki Blaze also visited people in their homes and talked about food, and music that resonated with 'home', which then culminated in a long table platform event where young people and community leaders came together to eat, share poetry and stories and debate the very present and challenging issues of housing.

The making of and performance of *She's Leaving Home* was a special process. The project was very specific to a community and a place and time, but hopefully the story of Kelsey is one that resonates and also feels universal.

She's Leaving Home was originally performed in a house in Toxteth Liverpool, as part of the fiftieth anniversary celebrations of *Sgt. Pepper's Lonely Hearts Club Band* in 2017. It also toured to a small number of other houses in the local community for audiences of the hosts' families and friends.

Kelsey	Brodie Arthur
Puppeteer	Zoe Hunter
Musician/Composer	Semay Wu

Writer and Musical Director   Keith Saha
Director   Julia Samuels
*Associate Direc*tor   Phelim McDermott
Puppetry Designer/Director   Alison Duddle
Dramaturg   Philip Osment
Producer   Amy Fisher
Production Manager   Richard Owen
Company Stage Managers   Bethany Sproston and Richard Owen
Associate Community Artists   Curtis Watt and Nikki Blaze

Big thanks to

Teresa MacDermott, Joe Farrag, Improbable, Claire McColgan MBE, Culture Liverpool, Liverpool City Council, 20 Stories High young participants, Curtis Watt, Nina Edge, Lisa Buckby, Anthony Proctor, Unity Theatre, Liverpool Housing Trust, Anita Welsh, Granby Four Street Market, Squash Nutrition, Toxteth TV, Kings Leadership Academy, Lizzie Nunnery, Lucy Graham, Clare Owens, Sarah Carroll, Jenny Growcoot, Laura Johnson, Tom Calderbank, Ami Yesufu, Daniel Houston, Pari Richards, Laura Connolly, Cherise Weaver, Sophie Holden, Daniel Simmons, Julie Kashirahanwe, Marije Michel, Jackie McGrath, Michael Allen, Anne-Marie Oliver, Roisin McKeon-Carter, Margaret Owen, Joanne Davis, LIPA and Selina Christy. *She's Leaving Home* Participation Programme and Platform Event: Our Lady of Mount Carmel Social Club, Rooftop Poets, Paul Holden, Pagoda Youth Orchestra, Kofi Owusu, Angelina Egeonu, Erroll Graham, Charlene Smith, Mandy Smith, Luise Watson and Aber Lighting.

Characters

Kelsey, *aged sixteen to twenty, dual heritage: black/white*
1960s Woman, *aged thirty, white*
Cellist
Reece, *aged twelve to sixteen: heard but not seen*

Note on Dialogue

When Kelsey's dialogue includes quotation marks, she is
reporting the words of other people in her story.

*The play is performed in a living room of a terraced house in Toxteth,
Liverpool. An audience of approximately ten people are invited to gather
outside and knock on the front door.*

1960s Woman *opens the front door, holding a feather duster, wearing a
yellow mini-dress and a pinny. She invites the audience into the house,
showing them through to the contemporary living room and offers them a
seat. She puts a Motown record on a portable record player, plumps the
cushions and continues her dusting. A* **Cellist***, with her instrument and
a loop pedal, sits in the corner watching.*

On the mantelpiece are an old school photograph of **Kelsey** *(aged six)
and her older sister Shannay (aged nine, dual heritage), a photograph of*
Reece *(thirteen, dual heritage) with his name engraved on the frame, and
a photo of Carter (three, white) also with his name on its frame. An
ornamental candle sits on the centre with the word 'mum'. There is a
snow globe with a Welsh dragon inside it. A pile of bills nestles behind it.*

*Scattered on a coffee table is an assortment of small plastic animals and
other toys. Next to it is a basket of clean washing.*

1960s Woman *reveals a toddler's painting. She shows it to the
audience and places it on the mantlepiece. At the top of the painting reads
the date 2013.*

Kelsey*, wearing her school uniform, passes the front window with a
bag of shopping and puts the key in the door.* **1960s Woman** *quickly
turns off the record player and sits down with the audience and waits . . .*

Scene One: 2013

4.30 p.m. From the front door, **Kelsey** *shouts across the street to a neighbour.*

Kelsey   Ahh, nice one, thanks Janeece, babes!
Do you wanna drop him off in about an hour . . . around sixish?
Well, I'll be in anyway so just giz a shout, if you need me!

No, it's okay, he can have his tea here . . .
Yeah . . . no . . . sound!
Alright Carter . . . are you going to blow you big sister a kiss?

Beat.

Caught it!
Now you be good . . . and no biting Dylan!

She enters the living room with a bag of shopping.

She puts the shopping bag down.

Reece?

She runs upstairs

Reece?

We hear the noise of Mario Kart 64 as she opens his bedroom door.

You alright, babe?
How was school? You got any homework?
Nice one . . .
No, I can't right now, babe,
I'll play you before I go out though . . .
What you going Donkey Kong for? He's too slow . . . you
    should go Toad
Hey you . . . I'm not a meff! You're a meff! You cheeky little get!

She runs downstairs.

She picks up the shopping and takes it into the kitchen.

She re-enters the living room, eating out of a large box of Rice Krispies.

She takes her tie and blazer off.

She gets out her GCSE Maths revision from her bag and places it on the table.

She starts to tidy up.

She half talks to herself.

Right, where am I up to?
Done the shopping.
Got the leccy.
Paid the broadband.
Washing . . . !

She looks directly at the audience.

Washing!
I'd forget my head if it wasn't screwed on.
Just pass us that basket, will yer?

She takes the basket from an audience member and starts to sort the washing.

Oh my God!
I am so excited . . . for tonight
I am proper pissing glitter!
It's my mate Teegan's sixteenth.
And her cousin's getting us all into the Camel Club, cos
    she knows the bouncers like.
She said in Science before, that all the Aigburth lads are going
    down as well.
You know, Paul and Donno and Jonnzi and all them lot?
But get on this . . .
She said Donno's bringing his cousin Femi from Tuebrook!
And I swear to God he is a proper hotty,
I seen him last year at the *Africa Oye,*[1]
And he's not one of them cocky ones that knows he's dead fit
    like, he's like, dead shy and cute!

1. *Africa Oye:* annual African musical festival.

Just how I like them.

Ha! What am I like?

It's gonna be well better than Gemma's sixteenth the other
    week . . .

She had it in the Caribbean . . .

The centre that is, not the islands!

Her Nan's goat curry was fit,

But her uncle was DJing and he was just playing all this . . .
    like . . . dead old skool . . . dance-hall . . . ragga stuff

And we was like can't you put something a bit more modern
    on, like Kano or Skepta or something?

But he didn't have any, so he just kept putting on 'Valerie' by
    Amy Winehouse which was good the first few times like,
    but we was dead sick of it by the end of the night.

He's ruined that song for me now, I'm telling you.

And then Teegan ended up spewing her ring by the end of
    the night cos she'd been drinking and had like *one* drag of
    a spliff!

Went on a proper whitey.

I said to her before, you best not be mixing your weed and ale
    tonight girl . . .

I don't wanna be scraping Nabzy's[2] out yer hair by the end
    of the night!

She finishes folding the washing.

God knows what I'm gonna do for my birthday like . . .

I'll probably just have a girls' night in with a DVD and some
    big bottles of WKD.

*She takes the basket of washing out of the living room and places it at the
bottom of the stairs.*

*She comes back in with a Primark bag, takes out a sparkly dress on
a hanger, and holds it against herself.*

What do you reckon?

I had to borrow it off my sister Shannay . . . do you think
    it's alright?

2. *Nabzy's:* a chicken shop.

I'm not sure . . .
Teegan's got a new dress from Top Shop
Honest to God, it's amazing . . . slits right up the sides, shows
    all of her back off and everything.
She's well gonna hog the limelight . . . The cow!
Well it is her birthday like, so I'll let her off this time.

She hangs the dress on the mantelpiece.

Just hang on a sec . . .

She leaves the room and takes the basket of washing upstairs.

She pokes her head into Reece's room.

Reece, what do you want for your tea, babe?

Do you want some spaghetti?

Alright, babes . . . I'll do it for six.

*She comes back down the stairs, and finishes tidying the living room,
removing the toys from the coffee table.*

I'll tell you what though . . . Our Shannay . . . when she
    dropped the dress off last night . . .
I swear down, she just attracts drama that girl!

She sits on back on the sofa.

It *was* lovely seeing our Lily though . . . that's me niece, our
    Shannay's little girl, she's getting proper big now . . . I can't
    believe it!
She was born prem you see . . . she's just gone three months
    now, but you'd think she was a newborn to look at her.
But I couldn't believe it . . .
Shannay said, that they might be getting evicted cos the
    landlord wants to move back in to his house, and he's only
    given them a month to find somewhere else!
And *then* . . . she says that they might have to come and live
    here for a bit, until they get themselves sorted?
And I'm like I'm not being funny or anything, Shannay but
    you can't!

Me mum's thinking of moving Derek in . . . things are starting
to get proper serious between them now!

And then she got a cob on and was like 'Why has no one
told me?'

And I was like, 'Well, why can't youse go and stay with Dozy
Dwayne's mum and dad in Speke?'

Dozy Dwayne's her fella. She hates it when I call him that!

'Dozy Dwayne the dodgy car dealer' . . . She swears down
his cars are legit . . . But there must be a reason why he
only sells them on Edgy[3] of a Sunday morning.

But then she was saying that she hates Speke cos it's too
white . . . and she wants to be nearer me and Mum . . .

She's on Kenny[4] at the minute.

And then for no reason, she just starts slagging Derek off,
calling him all sorts.

And I'm like, 'Hey you . . . leave him alone, what's he ever
done to you?'

My mum likes him and that's the main thing.

He's just what she needs at the minute.

And I'm not being sly, but they've hardly been queuing up
since our Carter's dad left.

Now he *was* a bastard.

Did one just after he was born.

I swear to God, Derek's like fucking Gandhi compared to him!

I said, 'Our Shannay, you should get yourself down the
housing and get yourself back on the Property Pool.'

But she was having none of it.

She blames the housing for our Lily being prem. You know
cos of the amount of stress they caused her.

She tried to get a place when she was three months pregnant,
but they said they couldn't give her anywhere until the baby
was actually born, until it had come out . . . and even then
it'd be somewhere like Crokky.[5]

So in the end, they had to go private.

Lot of fucking good, that did her!

3. *Edgy:* Edge Lane, a major road into Liverpool.
4. *Kenny:* Kensington, a road in Liverpool.
5. *Crokky:* Croxteth, a predominantly white area of Liverpool.

It'd be proper carnage if they moved back though.
It wouldn't work!
It'd set my mum right back!
She's only been back in the taxi rank, a couple of months . . .
And she's just starting to get back to her normal self again.

She's been laid up the past couple of years, cos of her back like,
    and it just made her proper miserable . . . hardly went out
    or spoke to anyone . . .
But you can't shut her up now!
Honest to God, she's worse than me,
Chews the ear off anyone who comes in the office,
That's how she met Derek . . . one of the regulars, uses the
    cabs to go to his Kennel Club meetings.
He breeds miniature Schnauzers. Calls them his *special little babies!*
I said to him . . . 'Oi, if you come and live here, don't be
    expecting me to clean up any of your Schnauzer shit. I've
    spent the past two years dealing with our Carter's shitty
    arse, I don't need any more!'
And that's another reason why I don't want her to come back!
You should have seen her last night!
She was like, 'Ahhh will you do our Lily's nappy for us, babes,
    I've just had my nails done!'
Princess frigging Shannay! I swear to God!
Me and my mum have always called her that.

Kelsey *gets her make-up bag from her schoolbag and empties the
contents on the table.*

*She begins to decide what products she will wear tonight, and tests them
on her hand.*

I tell you who would be happy if they come back though,
    Rita from next door.
She blames Dozy Dwayne for taking her away.
Cos he said to her once, that he didn't want to bring his kids
    up round here cos of all the tinned-up houses, and it looked
    like a war zone!
And there was proper murder! You know cos Rita's been the
    one campaigning for years to fix all the houses up like . . .

She was like, 'You should be wanting to bring your babies up in L8, bringing some life back to the place . . . not deserting us!'

She takes the dress off the mantelpiece and takes out her phone.

Just a sec.

She holds the dress against herself and takes a pouting selfie.

She glances out of the window at the boarded up houses.

I don't notice them to tell you the truth, they've been like that since I was born.

Her mobile phone vibrates.

Hang on a sec.

She answers it.

Hiya.
Yeah, I'm fine . . .
Yeah, I've done it . . .
A sixty degreer.
Yes I know, Mother!

Upstairs on his game.
No why?
No . . . I'm just about to . . .

He's over at Janeece's playing with Dylan . . .
No, go on, it's fine . . .

Ohhh. Right . . .
Okay . . .

So what time will you be back . . . is it a late one, like?
Oh . . . okay . . .

Yeah, I was supposed to be.
Teegan's sixteenth.
Yeah . . . tonight.

No, don't worry about it, it's fine.
No, it's fine . . . no, honestly . . .

You need the money.

I know there will be . . .

To tell you the truth . . . I was thinking of not going anyway.
Nah . . . Teegan's just been doing my head in.
You know what she's like, she can be a bit of diva.

Look, are you gonna manage to get something to eat?
Do you want me to save you some spaghetti for when you get
   in then?

Okay.
Go on then . . .

No, honestly, Mum. it's fine . . .
Shut up will yer?
Honest . . .
Honest to God . . .
I just said I was thinking of not going anyway . . . I just told
   you . . .
Go on then,
Alright
See you later . . .
Bye.

Gutted, she slowly puts the make-up away.

*She takes the dress off the mantelpiece, carefully folds it up and puts it
back in the Primark bag. She leaves it on the coffee table.*

She runs up the stairs to **Reece**'s *room.*

Reece! Come on then, mate. I'll have yer a game now
Right, 150cc?
Choco Mountain or Rainbow Road?
I tell you what . . . Why don't you go Princess Peach and I'll
   go Mario!
Ha! The look on your face!

The **Cellist** *begins to create a mournful but beautiful soundscape.*
1960s Woman *stands up, clears the Primark bag off the table, and
gently closes the door.*

She takes the toddler's painting off the mantelpiece and replaces it with a picture of a rainbow drawn by a slightly older child; the date on it reads 2015. She dusts the mantelpiece and adds more bills behind the snowglobe.

She dusts the table and pushes it forward. Under it, she discovers a sequin; she holds it up to the light; the music becomes hopeful.

She reaches into the Rice Krispies box and starts to eat the cereal out of her hand. She spreads it on the table and crushes it up, making a circle of dust.

She opens up the Rice Krispies box and it becomes a circus big top. Inside the box, sits an audience, who are paper cut outs of cultural icons from the 1960s to the present day, as well as people from **Kelsey***'s life. The music becomes reminiscent of a psychedelic circus.*

She removes a **Kelsey** *figure from the crowd and parades her around the circus, she gets the toy animals that she had tidied up previously and arranges them in the circus scene. From a shelf under the table she takes a tobacco tin, which she opens to reveal a cannon made out of a Rizla packet. She turns it into a circus act, firing more and more toys out of the cannon. Suddenly she hears the front door slam.*

1960s Woman *quickly shuts the Rice Krispies box, and sits down with the audience. The music stops.*

The room is a complete mess, Rice Krispies and toys are everywhere.

Scene Two: 2015

9 a.m. **Kelsey** *enters through the front door wearing a supermarket uniform.*

She enters the living room and sees the mess.

For fuck's sake! Arrrrrrgh!!!
Do you know anywhere that wants to house a Princess, a
    pot head and a frigging monster toddler?

She begins to tidy up. She goes into the kitchen, puts the kettle on and comes back with a dustpan and brush and begins to tidy up.

They've just gone into town to get our Lily a new pair of
    shoes this morning.
You'd have thought they could have tidied up before they went.
Honest to God . . . I've had enough of them!
I've just come back from taking our Carter to school.
I swear to God I hate that school.
As soon as I walk in they were like,
'We've noticed he still looks a bit peaky, are you sure he should
    be coming in?'
As if I can afford to take any more time of work!

She goes back into the kitchen with the dustpan and brush.

Great! Last friggin' tea bag and all!

We hear her make her cup of tea. Eventually, she comes back in.

Sorry, I'm down to my last teabag, so youse aren't getting one,
I'm afraid.

*She puts her mug down on the table, finishes tidying up, then sits on the
sofa.*

Her phone vibrates. It is a text from Femi.

Oh for fuck's sake! I've got enough little boys to look after
    with our Carter and our Reece, without Femi throwing his
    frigging toys out the pram.

She throws the phone down on the sofa.

He's only gone and frigging asked me to move in with him!
Last night . . . he invited me round for dinner . . .
Cos his mum was out . . .
And we'd both built it up to be dead special like, cos we've
    hardly been seeing each other . . . cos of his new job. And
    I've just had my head down with my A-levels and obviously
    running the show here!

And it started off sound, it was dead nice . . .
I was cooking his special jollof rice . . . nice bottle of wine . . .
    DVD . . .
The works . . . you know?

Felt like a proper special night.
And he was being dead lovely,
But then half way through the apple crumble
He just blurts out . . .
'I want you to move in with me.'

Beat.

And I was like, 'Are you fucking kidding me?
Are you being serious right now?'

I mean . . . of all the shitty-arse stunts to pull!

I was like, 'How do you think that that is even remotely
possible?
With everything I've got going on here.'
But he didn't get it.
He just pulled his sulky little boy face . . .

I can't be doing with it!

And then he was like . . . 'Do you not love me?'
And I said, 'Don't make this about you!'

'Of course I frigging love you . . . But that's not the point!'
And he was like, 'But that is the point cos if you did really
    love me then you'd move in with me!'
And I was like, 'No mate . . . sometimes you need to think
    about other people and put other people's needs first . . .
    not just your own!'
And then he had the cheek . . .
He had the cheek . . . to say that I do too much for other
    people and I need to start thinking about *myself.*
And I just seen him in this whole new light . . .
Selfish bastard.

We hear the noise of something landing through the letterbox.

Hang on a sec.

Kelsey *goes to the front door and comes back in, reading a postcard.*

Oh my God!
That's proper cute! Look at that!

It's from me mate Teegan!

She's just gone over to Dubai to teach English . . .

Lucky cow!

I'm always saying to my mum that we should all go away
  somewhere nice,

Abroad like.

And she's always like, *What's wrong with Rhyl?*

We go every year to see my nan.

And I'm like . . . 'I'm not gonna get to be the natural brown
  goddess I was destined to be . . . in frigging Rhyl, am I?'

But she's scared of flying.

I mean there was talk . . . once upon a time . . . of Derek
  taking us all to Disneyland Paris on the train.

But that's not gonna happen now, is it?

He ran off with the woman that used to shampoo and
  condition his Schnauzers!

Set up a salon together, and you'll never believe what they
  called it?

Doggy Style!

The dirty bastards.

She says she's over him like . . .

But I can tell she's still gutted.

I tried to get her to go on Match.com the other night

But she was like, 'What do I need a fella for, when I've got you?

You're my husband now, aren't you, babes?'

And I'm like . . . 'Ha . . . yeah, Mum . . . if you say so!'

I said to our Shannay, 'This is your fucking fault . . . If youse
  lot hadn't have grown roots here, they might have stood
  half a chance!'

Our Lily's just approaching her terrible twos having a tantrum
  every five minutes . . .

And Dwayne's mostly working away building up his *car empire*.

But when he is here they're either screaming blue murder
  or shagging.

You should have heard them last night. It was disgusting!

Sounded like frigging Pornhub . . . !

The kids shouldn't having to be hearing that!

Honest to God . . . The girl thinks she's Nikki frigging Minaj!

She reads the post card from Teegan and then puts it on the mantelpiece.

Ahhh, I'll have to Facetime her later to say thanks, I am proper
    made up for Teegan, though . . . she proper deserves it.
Me and Gemma have been offered a place at Salford in
    September to do business.
But I'm just gonna defer till next year . . .
I just need to chill for a bit . . . you know what I mean?

She gets another text.

Lad, why you being like that, when you know it's not even
    an option for me?
Sending me pictures of the frigging furniture!
Who does that?
It's just dead mean, innit?
Tempting someone with something you know that they can't
    have.
It's like shoving a big fuck off Costco cake in front of someone
    when you know they're on Slimming World.
Cos obviously I want to . . .
I love him to bits . . .
But I can't . . . not at the moment.

And his place is just gorgeous as well, honest to God!
You should see it.
His mum's going back to Nigeria you see, to open up a shop
And leaving him in charge of the place,
Which means we'd have it all to ourselves
But last night, you should have heard him . . .
He just kept on twisting the knife in, going on about how
    he's gonna do it all up . . .
With a new kitchen, new carpets, new double bed . . .
New sheets . . .
Yeah . . . he played that card an' all!
But I was having none of it.

And in the end, he just gave up and shut down
Wouldn't talk to me.

So I thought fuck this, I'm calling a Delta[6] . . .
And then as I was about to leave, he said what about
    Mrs Doubtfire?
I thought is he fucking serious?
As if I could snuggle up with him on the sofa and watch
    a DVD with him, after that!
He's never seen it before you see, and I've been going on
    about it for years cos it's one my favourites . . .
So I just said to him, 'I'll save you the trouble, babes.
He dresses up as a woman, his tits catch on fire, and by
    the end, he gets to see his kids.
And hashtag fucking spoiler alert, they all live happily ever after!'
And then I did one, and took the rice with me.
And left him snivelling on the sofa.

She checks her phone.

So now neither of us are saying sorry . . .

Have I been a bitch?
I have, haven't I?

I always do this . . .

I was like . . .
'Well, you should just fucking finish with me then! Cos
    obviously I can't give you what you want!
I know why don't you go and try your luck with Natalie,
    I'm sure she'd come and wash your fucking dishes and
    try out your new friggin' bed!'
Natalie's this girl he's just started working with . . .
I can be such bitch sometimes, I can't help myself.

She looks around at the mess.

I don't know . . .
Maybe there is a way . . .
Maybe . . . I could just stay weekends or something.
I'd have to ask our Shannay or Janeece to look after our
    Carter though.

6. *Delta:* a Liverpool minicab firm.

My mum would fucking flip though.
Last night when I got in . . . she was doing my head in.
She was like . . . 'What's up with your mug?'
But I couldn't tell her.
And she was like . . . 'I've told you before, babe, when you have
    murder with your fella, you just need to cut out the middle
    bit straight away . . . cos you've got to make up at some point!'
And I just said . . . 'Yeah . . . and that worked out fabulously
    for you and Derek didn't it, Mum?'
So now she's not talking to me either.

She stews.

Fuck her!
I'm gonna tell him to meet me in the Costa on Smithdown
    tonight after my shift. See if we can work it out . . .
Cos that kitchen . . . Honest to God!

She texts Femi back.

We hear the front door open and close, and footsteps running up the stairs.

Are you kidding me?
Not this again.
Hang on a sec.

She gets up and runs up the stairs.

Reece?
Reece?
What's going on?
Who was it this time?
Well, have you told anyone?
Did they hit you?
What did they do then?
You just need to learn to ignore them, what have I told you?
Do you *want* me mum to get another sixty-quid fine?
For fuck's sake!

She runs back downstairs, and looks at her phone.

Oh my God, look at the time! I've gotta go to work.

She puts her coat on and gets her bag ready.

Right, I'll see youse all in a bit.

She leaves the living room and shouts from the bottom of the stairs.

Reece . . .
I'm off to work now.
Make sure you give our Carter his tea when he gets home!
There's some left over jollof rice in the fridge for yers
And just make sure Posh and Becks don't eat any, they can get their own!
I've put a note on it, anyway!

And listen, babe, try not to worry about those dickheads . . . yeah?
It'll all work out in the end.

She exits through the front door. We see her walk past the front window.

1960s Woman *watches her walk down the street.*

*The **Cellist** creates a hopeful soundscape.*

1960s Woman *replaces the rainbow painting with a painting of a tiger by a slightly older child. The date reads 2017.*

She plumps the cushions on the sofa and sculpts them into a mountain range.

She finds a toy tiger down the side of the sofa.

The music becomes more dramatic.

She manipulates the tiger to make its way up the mountain range.

As it gets to the top, she picks up a nappy box from beside the sofa.

The music builds. Drum roll. The tiger jumps into the box. She closes the lid, and turns the box around to reveal a paper tiger trapped in a cage.

The tiger then turns into a washing machine on fire.

The music is dark.

*Suddenly we hear **Kelsey**'s voice from the back yard. The music stops.*

1960s Woman *sits down, taking the tiger and the box with her.*

Scene Three: 2017

5.30 p.m. **Kelsey** *enters from the back door, holding a tea-towel. She has pegs attached to the 'Subway' sandwich store uniform she is wearing. She is on the phone to her sister, mid-conversation.*

What do you mean 'What do *I* mean'?
Oh Shannay . . . you can fuck right off!
I didn't even hit her.

I don't care . . .
Put her on now.

She fucking pushed me!
You weren't even there . . .
How do you know?

Did I fuck?
I didn't.
Well, I didn't!
I didn't hit her . . . how many times?

I don't care what she's saying.
Cos she'd fucking know about it if I had!
Well, can you see any marks on her?
Well then . . .

Shannay, she pushed me!
So I slapped her back!
I couldn't help it, it was a reflex!
I *slapped* her . . . open palm . . . not a fist!

Well, she shouldn't have fucking pushed me then!
You didn't hear the way she was speaking to me!

Shannay, just put her the fuck on now!

Well, she needs to come home, I've got a shift starting in an hour.
Our Carter's in his room crying his frigging eyes out cos of it.
And God knows where our Reece is, I said I'd pick him up
    from school . . .
So he's probably on his way home now getting gay-bashed.

I'm not being dramatic . . . he's in the middle of his frigging
    GCSEs and I'm the one left to contend with all this!
Yet again!
You're the one causing unnecessary drama!

I didn't fucking hit her.

Why you taking her side? When you don't even know the facts.
I know she's stressed . . .
I'm frigging stressed, Our *Reece* is stressed . . . Our Carter's
    stressed . . .
Everyone's frigging stressed, Shannay . . .
But no!

It's not.
It's not an excuse . . .
You didn't hear the way she was . . .
Even Rita come round after she went, to see if *I* was okay!

How many more times?
I can't be arsed. Put her on the phone now!

I don't know . . . I can't even remember.
Something about how I'd shrunk the baby's pants and they'd
    come out the wash looking like dolls' pants . . .
And that I'd have to buy him a new pair . . .

Cos I can't friggin' afford it, Shannay!
No, I haven't got money *stashed* away!
Are you sure you wanna go there?
That's money I saved up for uni . . . you know that!

Well, what the fuck have you ever done apart from sit in
    your arse all day watching *Judge Rinder* and getting your
    nails done!

Yeah, well, I might go.
I might go to uni this year.
I might . . .

What the fuck do you know about it?
What the fuck have you ever contributed?

You was here for nearly two years and you didn't give my
    mum a bean!
I don't even know how you've got the nerve to call yourself
    a part of this family.

Cos you've just been a fucking sponge, that's why!

No, it's not just Dwayne's . . . It's your money as well, Shannay.
Yeah . . . Well, you might give her a bit now, but you never
    when you was staying here.
No you never.
No you never!
You never.
That is such a lie.
Go on . . . how much then?

What you lying for?
Well, she never told me about it.
Oh my God, so you saying me ma's a snide?
Yeah, you are, that's exactly what you're saying.
Cos I never seen a penny of it, and I've been doing
    the frigging books for God knows how many years!

Put her on . . . I want to speak to her now.

Yeah, well . . . Carry on like that girl, and I'll come over to
    Skem[7] and batter you myself . . . I don't care
    if you've just had a baby.

No, it's not Ormskirk, it's fucking Skem!
Why you always pretending to be something you're not?

Would you now?
Would you now?
Would you?
Would you?
Yeah, well I'd like to see you fucking try.
Yeah I frigging would!

7. *Skem:* Skelmersdale.

She throws the phone on the sofa and takes deep breaths.

She looks out of the window, calms herself down and picks up the phone, and dials.

She waits. Shannay answers.

Just tell her to come back home now, and stop acting like a kid!

Well, why did you pick up then?

Are you serious?
Youse are fucking off yer heads.
So what . . . ?
She's just leaving home then, is she?

I don't care if it's for one night or for one frigging year!
Tell her if she's not back by six
    I'm gonna grass her up to the social.

You just fucking watch me, girl!

I've gotta go to work!
How many more times?
Cos they're not my kids, Shannay!
I don't care if she can hear me . . .
I'm not a fucking superwoman!
Why can't youse understand that?
I can't do everything!

I know you've got your own kids!
But babes, I'm telling you, I can't cope any more!
Listen to me . . . listen to what I'm saying!
Cos you're just doing it as well!

Do people just look at me and see fucking mug written across
    my forehead?
I think they must do.
I think they must think . . . oh . . . here comes Kelsey Walker,
    frigging Mother Theresa!
They fucking do, Shannay!
Everyone does it!

My mum does it, you do it, Gemma does it, even Femi fucking
    used to do it!
Why do you think our relationship ended up being such
    a car crash?
'Let's ask Kelsey to do all the school runs, let's ask Kelsey to
    take Lily to the doctor's, let's ask Kelsey to borrow us
    another twenty quid, let's ask Kelsey to move in so she can
    be a friggin' replacement mother!'
Well, I'm not fucking doing it any more.
I've had enough, babes.
Honestly I have!
And you can tell her from me!
I've had enough.

Kelsey *hangs up the phone and breaks down.*

The **Cellist** *begins to respond musically to her mood.* **1960s Woman**
stands up and arranges the cushions around **Kelsey**. *She hangs a
washing line from one end of the room to the far corner. She produces a
puppet cardboard monkey on a unicycle and cycles it along the washing
line, as if it's on a tightrope.* **Kelsey** *stands up, she picks up the tea
towel.* **1960s Woman** *takes it from her and pegs it up on the washing
line.* **Kelsey** *picks up the photograph of her and Shannay from the
mantelpiece. She removes herself from the picture.* **1960s Woman**
hands **Kelsey** *a peg, and* **Kelsey** *pegs the picture of herself on the
line and replaces the photograph of an isolated Shannay back on the
mantelpiece. She leaves.*

1960s Woman *gets out a basket and pegs up an array of paper cut-
outs and real objects – a block of flats, a sock, a washing machine, a
black female pilot, a boarded-up row of houses, a female circus performer
carrying a tiger, a box of washing powder, a pair of dolls' pants, a
sparkly dress, a circus elephant, a black strongwoman, a trapeze artist.
She then takes Teegan's postcard of Dubai from the mantelpiece and pegs
that up. The music is beautiful and soaring. She takes out a cut-out of a
bird, which flies and swoops over the washing line. She then dances as she
folds the washing line away. The music fades; she sits down and waits.*

Scene Four: One Week Later

8.30 a.m. **Kelsey** *is in the hall. She opens the front door gently. She calls upstairs in hushed tones.*

Reece, Reece your taxi's here!

Reece *creeps down the stairs.*

Give me a hug.
Love you . . . babes.
Good luck in your French, hun.

Kelsey *shuts the front door.*

She enters the living room. She is wearing leggings and a T-shirt. She continues to talk in hushed tones.

My mum's still asleep.
Don't worry though, you won't wake her.
She's sleeping last night off.

She gets a small basket of clean washing and sits on the sofa. She starts to unpack the basket and fold the clothes into two piles on the coffee table.

Ahhh . . . it was dead nice last night . . . just what we needed.
My mum took us all down Lodgey[8] for a kebab.

And I was like, 'What's the special occasion?'
And she was like, 'No occasion;
    I just want to take youse all out . . . '
But I knew it was cos of what happened last week like.
You know . . .
The big kick off !

But it was boss you know . . .
We all had a proper laugh, it felt like Christmas . . .
She even ordered the banquet!
I was like . . . 'Oo-er! Someone's feeling flush!'

8. *Lodgey:* Lodge Lane, a road in Liverpool 8.

Our Shannay wasn't there . . . obviously.
But we Snapchatted her a picture.

And my mum was funny though, she just kept on ordering
    these bottles of wine . . .
And then she started pouring them into our Reece's 7-Up . . .
    making him frigging spritzers!
And I was like, 'Stop it, he's got his exams in the morning!'
But you should have seen him, he was proper tipsy, had us
    in bulk doing impressions of Rita and everything . . .
That lad, I'm telling yer!
But get on this, right.
Then he started saying about with how he fancies this lad in
    the sixth form and his name is Oscar!
Well, our jaws just fucking hit the floor!
Well, we knew he was gay like, he come out a couple of
    months ago . . .
But . . . we weren't expecting him to spill any beans like.
My mum was *beaming*, you should have seen her.
He said when he turns sixteen he's gonna take her down
    to Garlands[9] so she can relive her Cream[10] days.
Our Carter was made up an' all . . . seeing us all together.

She did come back . . . eventually like . . .
My mum, from our Shannay's.
She actually come back that night,
But . . . by the time she did
We was all in bed . . .

I'd given up on her to tell you the truth.

And for the next few days, we weren't really talking to each
    other . . .
We were like passing ships in the night anyway, cos of our
    shifts and that . . .
And I think it must have been Tuesday . . .

9. *Garlands:* a gay club in Liverpool.
10. *Cream:* Liverpool's now defunct super-club.

Tuesday dinner time . . .

Reece was in town shopping for his prom outfit and our
    Carter was in here watching his Paw Patrol.

And when I come in she was just sat at the kitchen table
    waiting for me.

And I thought . . . fucking hell . . . Here comes round two.

So I just blanked her and went to make a brew,

And she was like,

'Come and sit down for a minute will you, babe?'

And I was thinking . . . Oh God . . . what's she playing at?

But then when I went over . . .

I could see she'd been drawing on our Carter's little chalk
    board, and she'd started marking out this schedule.

Like a work plan thingy.

And in my head I thought . . . you can fuck right off,

I've been asking for one of them for years, and now there's
    been a kick-off she wants to make one?

And then she sat me down, and told me that she'd had word
    with her boss at work, to see how they could change her
    shifts around so she could be back for the school runs
    and that.

So I thought . . . go on then . . .

So she said how it's going to work . . .

Is that Janeece from over the road would take him every
    morning and pick up on a Monday, Tuesday, Wednesday

And then I could do it on Thursday and then my mum
    on Friday.

And I was like . . . 'Yeah . . . go on . . . that'll work.'

Then we started to work out the washing and the shopping,

And I was like, 'Well why can't we get our Reece to do it?'

And she was like, 'Our Reece? Are you kidding me?'

'He'll be ordering buckets of frigging frozen fried chicken.

'You know like them nasty ones you get from Iceland that
    pretend to be KFC but they're full of beaks?'

So then I was like, 'Well why don't we teach him how to use
    the washing machine?'

Cos he's always gotten out of doing the washing cos we
   think that cos he's a lad he's gonna fuck it up and ruin
   all our clothes . . .
But then we was thinking, well, if he can work out how to
   use the Firestick, and hack into the Netflix, then he should
   be tech savvy enough to work the fucking washer . . .
   I mean it's not rocket science is it?
But then we said we'd try him out on the baby's clothes for
   a bit, you know like a sort of a trial like . . .

And I knew I should have said sorry.
But I just couldn't.

And then she walked in here, and got to the door to go up
   and give Carter his bath, and I just walked over to her
   and put my arms around her and give her a big hug
And I said . . . 'I do love you, you know, Mum?'
And she was like, 'I know babe . . . I know.'
And then she started crying and I was like . . . 'Mum, don't
   cry . . . Mum please' . . .
And she hardly ever cries . . .
She only cries in films like *E.T.* or *Marley and Me*,
But never at . . . real stuff.

And we was just stood by the kitchen door . . . holding each
   other . . . rocking.
And then obviously that started me off.
And our Carter must have heard . . .
Cos he come in from his Paw Patrol.
And he marched over, and he was like . . . 'Why are youse sad?'
And my mum was like,' We're not sad babe . . . we're just
happy.'
And then he was like . . . 'Why, have youse had some wine?'
Ha!

She looks at the picture of Carter on the mantlepiece.

God, his eyes would melt you . . . he proper does feel like
   my baby though.

I know he's not like . . . I know he's my mum's obviously
  but I've spent as much time bringing him up . . .

It is dead calm round here now though.
Can you feel the calm?
It's been dead nice the past couple of days . . .

*She puts one of the two piles of washing back into the washing basket
and takes it to the kitchen.*

(*To herself.*) What the fuck am I doing?

She comes back in and sits back on the sofa.

You see last night after the kebab . . .
We was staggering back from Lodgey . . .
And me mum grabbed me at the top of the road
And she just whispered in my ear . . .
'You're still the best husband I've ever had you know.'
And I just knew it then . . .
I thought . . .
Yeah . . . I am
I am doing the right thing . . .

She picks up her phone and dials. She whispers.

Hya can I have a taxi please?
37 Beaconsfield.
John Lennon . . .
John Lennon Airport.
Thanks.

She puts phone down.

Bet you think I'm a right bitch now, don't you?

Beat.

The thing is, well the other day after me mum fucked off
  I just had no idea whether she was coming home or not, did I?
And I Facetimed my mate Teegan – do you know, the one who
  went to Dubai?
And I was in floods of tears and she was like . . .

'Come and stay over here with me?'
And I was like, 'What, for a holiday?'
And she was like, 'No come and live out here I know this
    woman who runs an agency, she'll be able to get you work
    and everything . . . It'll be boss.'
So
I just said 'Yeah' . . .
'Alright.'
And I got my passport and my tickets sorted the next day.

She gets up and quietly gets a suitcase from the hall.

*She places it on the coffee table, unzips it and packs the remaining pile of
clothes, which contains summer clothes, bikinis etc.*

I've just been shitting myself all week.
I haven't told anyone
    Apart from our Reece . . .
I told him on Monday after I got my passport sorted.
And I said to him, 'Listen, if you don't want me to go, I won't.'
But he was just like 'Get out, babe, as fast as you can, and don't
    look back.'
Sounds proper cheesy now like, but it wasn't when he said it.

Well . . . maybe it was a bit like,

Beat.

It's our Carter that I feel sly about though . . .
I know he'll be sound like.

She goes over to the mantelpiece and picks up his picture

But . . .
I'll just have to make sure that I Facetime him every day.

She places the picture in her suitcase.

Shit! I nearly forgot!

She goes to the kitchen and comes back with a box of Rice Krispies.

And crams it in her suitcase.

*The **Cellist** plays a beautiful slow and haunting version of The Beatles' 'She's Leaving Home'.*

Kelsey *zips up her suitcase. She gets a bill in an envelope from the mantelpiece, and searches in her bag for a pen.* **1960s Woman** *hands her one from her pinny.*

Kelsey *writes on the back of the envelope a letter to her mum, as the music builds.*

This is written for the audience to see, not *to be read aloud.*

Dear Mum

I love you more than anything in the world
I'm so sorry I couldn't say goodbye
I'll ring you in a few days
I just need to get away for a bit.
And have some space and time for myself.
I think you are the best mum ever.
Love you always

Kelz Belz
xxxxxxxxxxxx

She gets one hundred pounds out of her purse and puts it inside the envelope.

She puts the envelope on the mantelpiece for the audience to read.

She sits on the sofa and waits for the taxi.

And waits . . .

The music continues.

Kelsey *checks her bag to make sure she's got her passport and documents. She puts on her jacket. She checks her pockets and removes a box of matches from one of them, leaving it on the coffee table.*

A taxi pulls up outside the house. It beeps its horn twice. **Kelsey** *stands up.*

Right . . . that's me

Beat.

In a bit.

She exits through the front door with her suitcase.

1960s Woman *and the audience watch* **Kelsey** *get into the taxi and drive off down the street.*

1960s Woman *picks up the matchbox and peeks inside. She closes the box again and gives it to an audience member to pass around. She leaves the room.*

Inside the box is a collage with a paper cut-out of **Kelsey** *with butterfly wings. walking down a street of semi boarded-up houses.*

The **Cellist** *finishes playing, and leaves through the back door.*

The End.

For a complete listing of Bloomsbury
Methuen Drama titles, visit:

www.bloomsbury.com/drama

Follow us on Twitter and keep up to date
with our news and publications

@MethuenDrama